MY CAKE AND BAKE COOKBOOK 2021

A SELECTION OF TASTY RECIPES FOR EVERY OCCASION

PAULINE POWELL

Table of Contents

Oat and Raisin Cookies

Makes 20

175 g/6 oz/¾ cup plain (all-purpose) flour

150 g/5 oz/1¼ cups rolled oats

5 ml/1 tsp ground ginger

2.5 ml/½ tsp baking powder

2.5 ml/½ tsp bicarbonate of soda (baking soda)

100 g/4 oz/½ cup soft brown sugar

50 g/2 oz/1/3 cup raisins

1 egg, lightly beaten

150 ml/¼ pt/2/3 cup oil

60 ml/4 tbsp milk

Mix together the dry ingredients, stir in the raisins and make a well in the centre. Add the egg, oil and milk and mix to a soft dough. Place spoonfuls of the mixture on an ungreased baking (cookie) sheet and flatten slightly with a fork. Bake in a preheated oven at 200°C/400°F/ gas mark 6 for 10 minutes until golden.

Spiced Oatmeal Biscuits

Makes 30

100 g/4 oz/½ cup butter or margarine, softened

100 g/4 oz/½ cup soft brown sugar

100 g/4 oz/½ cup caster (superfine) sugar

1 egg

2.5 ml/½ tsp vanilla essence (extract)

100 g/4 oz/1 cup plain (all-purpose) flour

2.5 ml/½ tsp bicarbonate of soda (baking soda)

A pinch of salt

5 ml/1 tsp ground cinnamon

A pinch of grated nutmeg

100 g/4 oz/1 cup rolled oats

50 g/2 oz/½ cup chopped mixed nuts

50 g/2 oz/½ cup chocolate chips

Cream together the butter or margarine and sugars until light and fluffy. Gradually beat in the egg and vanilla essence. Mix together the flour, bicarbonate of soda, salt and spices and add to the mixture. Stir in the oats, nuts and chocolate chips. Drop rounded teaspoonfuls on to a greased baking (cookie) sheet and bake the biscuits (cookies) in a preheated oven at 180°C/ 350°F/gas mark 4 for 10 minutes until lightly browned.

Wholemeal Oat Biscuits

Makes 24

100 g/4 oz/½ cup butter or margarine

200 g/7 oz/1¾ cups oatmeal

75 g/3 oz/¾ cup wholemeal (wholewheat) flour

50 g/2 oz/½ cup plain (all-purpose) flour

5 ml/1 tsp baking powder

50 g/2 oz/¼ cup demerara sugar

1 egg, lightly beaten

30 ml/2 tbsp milk

Rub the butter or margarine into the oatmeal, flours and baking powder until the mixture resembles breadcrumbs. Stir in the sugar, then mix in the egg and milk to make a stiff dough. Roll out the dough on a lightly floured surface to about 1 cm/½ in thick and cut into rounds with a 5 cm/2 in cutter. Place the biscuits (cookies) on a greased baking (cookie) sheet and bake in a preheated oven at 190°C/375°F/gas mark 5 for about 15 minutes until golden brown.

Orange Biscuits

Makes 24

100 g/4 oz/½ cup butter or margarine, softened

50 g/2 oz/¼ cup caster (superfine) sugar

Grated rind of 1 orange

150 g/5 oz/1¼ cups self-raising (self-rising) flour

Cream together the butter or margarine and sugar until light and fluffy. Work in the orange rind, then mix in the flour to make a stiff mixture. Shape into large walnut-sized balls and arrange well apart on a greased baking (cookie) sheet, then press down lightly with a fork to flatten. Bake the biscuits (cookies) in a preheated oven at 180°C/350°F/gas mark 4 for 15 minutes until golden brown.

Orange and Lemon Biscuits

Makes 30

50 g/2 oz/¼ cup butter or margarine, softened

75 g/3 oz/1/3 cup caster (superfine) sugar

1 egg yolk

Grated rind of ½ orange

15 ml/1 tbsp lemon juice

150 g/5 oz/1¼ cups plain (all-purpose) flour

2.5 ml/½ tsp baking powder

A pinch of salt

Cream together the butter or margarine and sugar until light and fluffy. Gradually mix in the egg yolk, orange rind and lemon juice, then fold in the flour, baking powder and salt to make a stiff dough. Wrap and clingfilm (plastic wrap) and chill for 30 minutes.

Roll out on a lightly floured surface to about 5 mm/¼ in thick and cut into shapes with a biscuit (cookie) cutter. Place the biscuits on a greased baking (cookie) sheet and bake in a preheated oven at 190°C/375°F/gas mark 5 for 10 minutes.

Orange and Walnut Biscuits

Makes 16

100 g/4 oz/½ cup butter or margarine

75 g/3 oz/1/3 cup caster (superfine) sugar

Grated rind of ½ orange

150 g/5 oz/1¼ cups self-raising (self-rising) flour

50 g/2 oz/½ cup walnuts, ground

Beat the butter or margarine with 50 g/2 oz/¼ cup of the sugar and the orange rind until smooth and creamy. Add the flour and nuts and beat again until the mixture begins to hold together. Form into balls and flatten on to a greased baking (cookie) sheet. Bake the biscuits (cookies) in a preheated oven at 190°C/ 375°F/gas mark 5 for 10 minutes until brown round the edges. Sprinkle with the reserved sugar and leave to cool slightly before transferring to a wire rack to cool.

Orange and Chocolate Chip Biscuits

Makes 30

50 g/2 oz/¼ cup butter or margarine, softened

75 g/3 oz/1/3 cup lard (shortening)

175 g/6 oz/¾ cup soft brown sugar

100 g/7 oz/1¾ cups wholemeal (wholewheat) flour

75 g/3 oz/¾ cup ground almonds

10 ml/2 tsp baking powder

75 g/3 oz/¾ cup chocolate drops

Grated rind of 2 oranges

15 ml/1 tbsp orange juice

1 egg

Caster (superfine) sugar for sprinkling

Cream together the butter or margarine, lard and brown sugar until light and fluffy. Add the remaining ingredients except the caster sugar and mix to a dough. Roll out on a floured surface to 5 mm/¼ in thick and cut into biscuits with a biscuit (cookie) cutter. Arrange on a greased baking (cookie) sheet and bake in a preheated oven at 180°C/350°F/gas mark 4 for 20 minutes until golden.

Spiced Orange Biscuits

Makes 10

225 g/8 oz/2 cups plain (all-purpose) flour

2.5 ml/½ tsp ground cinnamon

A pinch of mixed (apple pie) spice

75 g/3 oz/1/3 cup caster (superfine) sugar

150 g/5 oz/2/3 cup butter or margarine, softened

2 egg yolks

Grated rind of 1 orange

75 g/3 oz/¾ cup plain (semi-sweet) chocolate

Mix together the flour and spices, then stir in the sugar. Beat in the butter or margarine, egg yolks and orange rind and mix to a smooth dough. Wrap in clingfim (plastic wrap) and chill for 1 hour.

Spoon the dough into a piping bag fitted with a large star nozzle (tip) and pipe lengths on to a greased baking (cookie) sheet. Bake in a preheated oven at 190°C/375°F/gas mark 5 for 10 minutes until golden brown. Leave to cool.

Melt the chocolate in a heatproof bowl set over a pan of gently simmering water. Dip the ends of the biscuits into the melted chocolate and leave on a sheet of baking parchment until set.

Peanut Butter Biscuits

Makes 18

100 g/4 oz/½ cup butter or margarine, softened

100 g/4 oz/½ cup caster (superfine) sugar

100 g/4 oz/½ cup crunchy or smooth peanut butter

60 ml/4 tbsp golden (light corn) syrup

15 ml/1 tbsp milk

175 g/6 oz/1½ cups plain (all-purpose) flour

2.5 ml/½ tsp bicarbonate of soda (baking soda)

Cream together the butter or margarine and sugar until light and fluffy. Blend in the peanut butter, followed by the syrup and milk. Mix together the flour and bicarbonate of soda and blend into the mixture, then knead until smooth. Shape into a log and chill until firm.

Cut into slices 5 mm/¼ in thick and arrange on a lightly greased baking (cookie) sheet. Bake the biscuits (cookies) in a preheated oven at 180°C/350°F/gas mark 4 for 12 minutes until golden.

Peanut Butter and Chocolate Swirls

Makes 24

50 g/2 oz/¼ cup butter or margarine, softened

50 g/2 oz/¼ cup soft brown sugar

50 g/2 oz/¼ cup caster (superfine) sugar

50 g/2 oz/¼ cup smooth peanut butter

1 egg yolk

75 g/3 oz/¾ cup plain (all-purpose) flour

2.5 ml/½ tsp bicarbonate of soda (baking soda)

50 g/2 oz/½ cup plain (semi-sweet) chocolate

Cream together the butter or margarine and sugars until light and fluffy. Gradually blend in the peanut butter, then the egg yolk. Mix together the flour and bicarbonate of soda and beat into the mixture to make a firm dough. Meanwhile, melt the chocolate in a heatproof bowl set over a pan of gently simmering water. Roll out the dough to 30 x 46 cm/12 x 18 in and spread with the melted chocolate almost to the edges. Roll up from the long side, wrap in clingfilm (plastic wrap) and chill until firm.

Cut the roll into 5 mm/¼ in slices and arrange on an ungreased baking (cookie) sheet. Bake in a preheated oven at 180°C/350°F/gas mark 4 for 10 minutes until golden.

Oaty Peanut Butter Biscuits

Makes 24

75 g/3 oz/1/3 cup butter or margarine, softened

75 g/3 oz/1/3 cup peanut butter

150 g/5 oz/2/3 cup soft brown sugar

1 egg

50 g/2 oz/½ cup plain (all-purpose) flour

2.5 ml/½ tsp baking powder

A pinch of salt

A few drops of vanilla essence (extract)

75 g/3 oz/¾ cup rolled oats

40 g/1½ oz/1/3 cup chocolate chips

Cream together the butter or margarine, peanut butter and sugar until light and fluffy. Gradually beat in the egg. Fold in the flour, baking powder and salt. Stir in the vanilla essence, oats and chocolate chips. Drop spoonfuls on to a greased baking (cookie) sheet and bake the biscuits (cookies) in a preheated oven at 180°C/350°F/gas mark 4 for 15 minutes.

Honey and Coconut Peanut Butter Biscuits

Makes 24

120 ml/4 fl oz/½ cup oil

175 g/6 oz/½ cup clear honey

175 g/6 oz/¾ cup crunchy peanut butter

1 egg, beaten

100 g/4 oz/1 cup rolled oats

225 g/8 oz/2 cups wholemeal (wholewheat) flour

50 g/2 oz/½ cup desiccated (shredded) coconut

Mix together the oil, honey, peanut butter and egg, then stir in the remaining ingredients. Drop spoonfuls on to a greased baking (cookie) sheet and flatten slightly to about 6 mm/¼ in thick. Bake the biscuits (cookies) in a preheated oven at 180°C/350°F/gas mark 4 for 12 minutes until golden.

Pecan Nut Biscuits

Makes 24

100 g/4 oz/½ cup butter or margarine, softened

45 ml/3 tbsp soft brown sugar

100 g/4 oz/1 cup plain (all-purpose) flour

A pinch of salt

5 ml/1 tsp vanilla essence (extract)

100 g/4 oz/1 cup pecan nuts, finely chopped

Icing (confectioners') sugar, sifted, for dusting

Cream together the butter or margarine and sugar until light and fluffy. Gradually beat in the remaining ingredients except the icing sugar. Shape into 3 cm/1½ in balls and arrange on a greased baking (cookie) sheet. Bake the biscuits (cookies) in a preheated oven at 160°C/325°F/gas mark 3 for 15 minutes until golden. Serve dusted with icing sugar.

Pinwheel Biscuits

Makes 24

175 g/6 oz/1½ cups plain (all-purpose) flour

5 ml/1 tsp baking powder

A pinch of salt

75 g/3 oz/1/3 cup butter or margarine

75 g/3 oz/1/3 cup caster (superfine) sugar

A few drops of vanilla essence (extract)

20 ml/4 tsp water

10 ml/2 tsp cocoa (unsweetened chocolate) powder

Mix together the flour, baking powder and salt, then rub in the butter or margarine until the mixture resembles breadcrumbs. Stir in the sugar. Add the vanilla essence and water and mix to a smooth dough. Shape into a ball, then cut in half. Work the cocoa into one half of the dough. Roll out each piece of dough to a 25 x 18 cm/10 x 7 in rectangle and place one on top of the other. Roll gently so they stick together. Roll up the dough from the long side and press together gently. Wrap in clingfilm (plastic wrap) and chill for about 30 minutes.

Cut into slices 2.5 cm/1 in thick and arrange, well apart, on a greased baking (cookie) sheet. Bake the biscuits (cookies) in a preheated oven at 180°C/350°F/gas mark 4 for 15 minutes until golden.

Quick Buttermilk Biscuits

Makes 12

75 g/3 oz/1/3 cup butter or margarine

225 g/8 oz/2 cups plain (all-purpose) flour

15 ml/1 tbsp baking powder

2.5 ml/½ tsp salt

175 ml/6 fl oz/¾ cup buttermilk

Icing (confectioners') sugar, sifted, for dusting (optional)

Rub the butter or margarine into the flour, baking powder and salt until the mixture resembles breadcrumbs. Gradually add the buttermilk to make a soft dough. Roll out the mixture on a lightly floured surface to about 2 cm/¾ in thick and cut into rounds with a biscuit (cookie) cutter. Place the biscuits on a greased baking (cookie) sheet and bake in a preheated oven at 230°C/450°F/gas mark 8 for 10 minutes until golden brown. Dust with icing sugar, if liked.

Raisin Biscuits

Makes 24

100 g/4 oz/½ cup butter or margarine, softened

50 g/2 oz/¼ cup caster (superfine) sugar

Grated rind of 1 lemon

50 g/2 oz/1/3 cup raisins

150 g/5 oz/1¼ cups self-raising (self-rising) flour

Cream together the butter or margarine and sugar until light and fluffy. Work in the lemon rind, then mix in the raisins and flour to make a stiff mixture. Shape into large walnut-sized balls and arrange well apart on a greased baking (cookie) sheet, then press down lightly with a fork to flatten. Bake the biscuits (cookies) in a preheated oven at 180°C/350°F/gas mark 4 for 15 minutes until golden brown.

Soft Raisin Biscuits

Makes 36

100 g/4 oz/2/3 cup raisins

90 ml/6 tbsp boiling water

50 g/2 oz/¼ cup butter or margarine, softened

175 g/6 oz/¾ cup caster (superfine) sugar

1 egg, lightly beaten

2.5 ml/½ tsp vanilla essence (extract)

175 g/6 oz/1½ cups plain (all-purpose) flour

2.5 ml/½ tsp baking powder

1.5 ml/¼ tsp bicarbonate of soda (baking soda)

2.5 ml/½ tsp salt

2.5 ml/½ tsp ground cinnamon

A pinch of grated nutmeg

50 g/2 oz/½ cup chopped mixed nuts

Place the raisins and boiling water in a pan, bring to the boil, cover and simmer for 3 minutes. Leave to cool. Cream together the butter or margarine and sugar until light and fluffy. Gradually beat in the egg and vanilla essence. Fold in the flour, baking powder, bicarbonate of soda, salt and spices alternately with the raisins and soaking liquid. Stir in the nuts and mix to a soft dough. Wrap in clingfilm (plastic wrap) and chill for at least 1 hour.

Drop spoonfuls of dough on to a greased baking (cookie) sheet and bake the biscuits (cookies) in a preheated oven at 180°C/350°F/gas mark 4 for 10 minutes until golden.

Raisin and Treacle Slices

Makes 24

25 g/1 oz/2 tbsp butter or margarine, softened

100 g/4 oz/½ cup caster (superfine) sugar

1 egg yolk

30 ml/2 tbsp black treacle (molasses)

75 g/3 oz/½ cup currants

150 g/5 oz/1¼ cups plain (all-purpose) flour

5 ml/1 tsp bicarbonate of soda (baking soda)

5 ml/1 tsp ground cinnamon

A pinch of salt

30 ml/2 tbsp cold black coffee

Cream together the butter or margarine and sugar until light and fluffy. Gradually beat in the egg yolk and treacle, then stir in the currants. Mix together the flour, bicarbonate of soda, cinnamon and salt and stir into the mixture with the coffee. Cover and chill the mixture.

Roll out to a 30 cm/12 in square, then roll up into a log. Place on a greased baking (cookie) sheet and bake in a preheated oven at 180°C/350°F/gas mark 4 for 15 minutes until firm to the touch. Cut into slices, then leave to cool on a wire rack.

Ratafia Biscuits

Makes 16

100 g/4 oz/½ cup granulated sugar

50 g/2 oz/¼ cup ground almonds

15 ml/1 tbsp ground rice

1 egg white

25 g/1 oz/¼ cup flaked (slivered) almonds

Blend together the sugar, ground almonds and ground rice. Beat in the egg white and continue to beat for 2 minutes. Pipe walnut-sized biscuits (cookies) on to a baking (cookie) sheet lined with rice paper using a 5 mm/¼ in plain nozzle (tip). Place a flaked almond on top of each biscuit. Bake in a preheated oven at 190°C/375°F/gas mark 5 for 15 minutes until golden.

Rice and Muesli Cookies

Makes 24

75 g/3 oz/¼ cup cooked brown rice

50 g/2 oz/½ cup muesli

75 g/3 oz/¾ cup wholemeal (wholewheat) flour

2.5 ml/½ tsp salt

2.5 ml/½ tsp bicarbonate of soda (baking soda)

5 ml/1 tsp ground mixed (apple pie) spice

30 ml/2 tbsp clear honey

75 g/3 oz/1/3 cup butter or margarine, softened

Mix together the rice, muesli, flour, salt, bicarbonate of soda and mixed spice. Cream together the honey and butter or margarine until soft. Beat into the rice mixture. Shape the mixture into walnut-sized balls and place well apart on greased baking (cookie) sheets. Flatten slightly, then bake in a preheated oven at 190°C/375°F/gas mark 5 for 15 minutes or until golden brown. Leave to cool for 10 minutes, then transfer to a wire rack to finish cooling. Store in an airtight container.

Romany Creams

Makes 10

25 g/1 oz/2 tbsp lard (shortening)

25 g/1 oz/2 tbsp butter or margarine, softened

50 g/2 oz/¼ cup soft brown sugar

2.5 ml/½ tsp golden (light corn) syrup

50 g/2 oz/½ cup plain (all-purpose) flour

A pinch of salt

25 g/1 oz/¼ cup rolled oats

2.5 ml/½ tsp ground mixed (apple-pie) spice

2.5 ml/½ tsp bicarbonate of soda (baking soda)

10 ml/2 tsp boiling water

Butter Icing

Cream together the lard, butter or margarine and sugar until light and fluffy. Beat in the syrup, then add the flour, salt, oats and mixed spice and stir until well blended. Dissolve the bicarbonate of soda in the water and mix in to make a firm dough. Shape into 20 equal-sized small balls and place well apart on greased baking (cookie) sheets. Flatten slightly with the palm of your hand. Bake in a preheated oven at 160°C/325°F/gas mark 3 for 15 minutes. Leave to cool on the baking sheets. When cool, sandwich pairs of biscuits together with the butter icing (frosting).

Sand Biscuits

Makes 48

100 g/4 oz/½ cup butter or hard margarine, softened

225 g/8 oz/1 cup soft brown sugar

1 egg, lightly beaten

225 g/8 oz/2 cups plain (all-purpose) flour

Egg white to glaze

30 ml/2 tbsp crushed peanuts

Cream together the butter or margarine and sugar until light and fluffy. Beat in the egg, then blend in the flour. Roll out very thinly on a lightly floured surface and cut into shapes with a biscuit (cookie) cutter. Place the biscuits on a greased baking (cookie) sheet, brush the tops with egg white and sprinkle with peanuts. Bake in a preheated oven at 180°C/350°F/gas mark 4 for 10 minutes until golden.

Soured Cream Cookies

Makes 24

50 g/2 oz/¼ cup butter or margarine, softened

175 g/6 oz/¾ cup caster (superfine) sugar

1 egg

60 ml/4 tbsp soured (dairy sour) cream

2. 5 ml/½ tsp vanilla essence (extract)

150 g/5 oz/1¼ cups plain (all-purpose) flour

2.5 ml/½ tsp baking powder

75 g/3 oz/½ cup raisins

Cream together the butter or margarine and sugar until light and fluffy. Gradually beat in the egg, cream and vanilla essence. Mix together the flour, baking powder and raisins and stir into the mixture until well blended. Drop rounded teaspoonfuls of the mixture on to lightly greased baking (cookie) sheets and bake in a preheated oven at 180°C/ 350°F/gas mark 4 for about 10 minutes until just golden.

Brown Sugar Biscuits

Makes 24

100 g/4 oz/½ cup butter or margarine, softened

100 g/4 oz/½ cup soft brown sugar

1 egg, lightly beaten

2.5 ml/1 tsp vanilla essence (extract)

150 g/5 oz/1¼ cups plain (all-purpose) flour

2.5 ml/½ tsp bicarbonate of soda (baking soda)

A pinch of salt

75 g/3 oz/½ cup sultanas (golden raisins)

Cream together the butter or margarine and sugar until light and fluffy. Gradually beat in the egg and vanilla essence. Stir in the remaining ingredients until smooth. Drop rounded teaspoonfuls well apart on to a lightly greased baking (cookie) sheet. Bake the biscuits (cookies) in a preheated oven at 180°C/ 350°F/gas mark 4 for 12 minutes until golden brown.

Sugar and Nutmeg Biscuits

Makes 24

50 g/2 oz/¼ cup butter or margarine, softened

100 g/4 oz/½ cup caster (superfine) sugar

1 egg yolk

2.5 ml/½ tsp vanilla essence (extract)

150 g/5 oz/1¼ cups plain (all-purpose) flour

5 ml/1 tsp baking powder

A pinch of grated nutmeg

60 ml/4 tbsp soured (dairy sour) cream

Cream together the butter or margarine and sugar until light and fluffy. Beat in the egg yolk and vanilla essence, then stir in the flour, baking powder and nutmeg. Blend in the cream until smooth. Cover and chill for 30 minutes.

Roll out the dough to 5 mm/¼ in thick and cut into 5 cm/2 in rounds with a biscuit (cookie) cutter. Place the biscuits on an ungreased baking (cookie) sheet and bake in a preheated oven at 200°C/ 400°F/gas mark 6 for 10 minutes until golden.

Shortbread

Makes 8

150 g/5 oz/1¼ cups plain (all-purpose) flour

A pinch of salt

25 g/1 oz/¼ cup rice flour or ground rice

50 g/2 oz/¼ cup caster (superfine) sugar

100 g/4 oz/¼ cup butter or hard margarine, chilled and grated

Mix together the flour, salt and rice flour or ground rice. Stir in the sugar, then the butter or margarine. Work the mixture with the fingertips until it resembles breadcrumbs. Press into an 18 cm/7 in sandwich tin (pan) and level the top. Prick all over with a fork and mark into eight equal wedges, cutting through to the base. Chill for 1 hour.

Bake in a preheated oven at 150°C/ 300°F/gas mark 2 for 1 hour until pale straw-coloured. Leave to cool in the tin before turning out.

Christmas Shortbread

Makes 12

175 g/6 oz/¾ cup butter or margarine

250 g/9 oz/2¼ cups plain (all-purpose) flour

75 g/3 oz/1/3 cup caster (superfine) sugar

For the topping:

15 ml/1 tbsp almonds, chopped

15 ml/1 tbsp walnuts, chopped

30 ml/2 tbsp raisins

30 ml/2 tbsp glacé (candied) cherries, chopped

Grated rind of 1 lemon

15 ml/1 tbsp caster (superfine) sugar for sprinkling

Rub the butter or margarine into the flour until the mixture resembles breadcrumbs. Stir in the sugar. Press the mixture together to a paste and knead until smooth. Press into a greased Swiss roll tin (jelly roll pan) and level the surface. Mix together the topping ingredients and press them into the paste. Mark into 12 fingers, then bake in a preheated oven at 180°C/350°F/gas mark 4 for 30 minutes. Sprinkle with caster sugar, cut into fingers and leave to cool in the tin.

Honeyed Shortbread

Makes 12

100 g/4 oz/½ cup butter or margarine, softened

75 g/3 oz/¼ cup set honey

200 g/7 oz/1¾ cups wholemeal (wholewheat) flour

25 g/1 oz/¼ cup brown rice flour

Grated rind of 1 lemon

Cream together the butter or margarine and honey until soft. Stir in the flours and lemon rind and work to a soft dough. Press into a greased and floured 18 cm/7 in cake tin (pan) or shortbread mould and prick all over with a fork. Mark into 12 wedges and crimp the edges. Chill for 1 hour.

Bake in a preheated oven at 150°C/ 300°F/gas mark 2 for 40 minutes until just golden. Cut into the marked pieces and leave to cool in the tin.

Lemon Shortbread

Makes 12

100 g/4 oz/1 cup plain (all-purpose) flour

50 g/2 oz/½ cup cornflour (cornstarch)

100 g/4 oz/½ cup butter or margarine, softened

50 g/2 oz/¼ cup caster (superfine) sugar

Grated rind of 1 lemon

Caster (superfine) sugar for sprinkling

Sift the flour and cornflour together. Cream the butter or margarine until soft, then beat in the caster sugar until pale and fluffy. Stir in the lemon rind, then beat in the flour mixture until well blended. Roll out the shortbread to a 20 cm/8 in circle and place on a greased baking (cookie) sheet. Prick all over with a fork and flute the edges. Cut into 12 wedges, then sprinkle with caster sugar. Chill in the fridge for 15 minutes. Bake in a preheated oven at 160°C/325°F/gas mark 3 for 35 minutes until pale golden brown. Leave to cool on the baking sheet for 5 minutes before turning out on to a wire rack to finish cooling.

Mincemeat Shortbread

Makes 8

175 g/6 oz/¾ cup butter or margarine, softened

50 g/2 oz/¼ cup caster (superfine) sugar

225 g/8 oz/2 cups plain (all-purpose) flour

60 ml/4 tbsp mincemeat

Cream the butter or margarine and sugar until soft. Work in the flour, then the mincemeat. Press into a 23 cm/ 7 in sandwich tin and level the top. Prick all over with a fork and mark into eight wedges, cutting through to the base. Chill for 1 hour.

Bake in a preheated oven at 160°C/ 325°F/gas mark 3 for 1 hour until pale straw-coloured. Leave to cool in the tin before turning out.

Nut Shortbread

Makes 12

100 g/4 oz/½ cup butter or margarine, softened

50 g/2 oz/¼ cup caster (superfine) sugar

100 g/4 oz/1 cup plain (all-purpose) flour

50 g/2 oz/½ cup ground rice

50 g/2 oz/½ cup almonds, finely chopped

Beat together the butter or margarine and sugar until light and fluffy. Mix in the flour and ground rice. Stir in the nuts and mix to a firm dough. Knead lightly until smooth. Press into the base of a greased Swiss roll tin (jelly roll pan) and level the surface. Prick all over with a fork. Bake in a preheated oven at 160°C/325°F/ gas mark 3 for 45 minutes until pale golden brown. Leave to cool in the tin for 10 minutes, then cut into fingers. Leave in the tin to finish cooling before turning out.

Orange Shortbread

Makes 12

100 g/4 oz/1 cup plain (all-purpose) flour

50 g/2 oz/½ cup cornflour (cornstarch)

100 g/4 oz/½ cup butter or margarine, softened

50 g/2 oz/¼ cup caster (superfine) sugar

Grated rind of 1 orange

Caster (superfine) sugar for sprinkling

Sift the flour and cornflour together. Cream the butter or margarine until soft, then beat in the caster sugar until pale and fluffy. Stir in the orange rind, then beat in the flour mixture until well blended. Roll out the shortbread to a 20 cm/8 in circle and place on a greased baking (cookie) sheet. Prick all over with a fork and flute the edges. Cut into 12 wedges, then sprinkle with caster sugar. Chill in the fridge for 15 minutes. Bake in a preheated oven at 160°C/325°F/gas mark 3 for 35 minutes until pale golden brown. Leave to cool on the baking sheet for 5 minutes before turning out on to a wire rack to finish cooling.

Rich Man's Shortbread

Makes 36

For the base:
225 g/8 oz/1 cup butter or margarine

275 g/10 oz/2½ cups plain (all-purpose) flour

100 g/4 oz/½ cup caster (superfine) sugar

For the filling:
225 g/8 oz/1 cup butter or margarine

225 g/8 oz/1 cup soft brown sugar

60 ml/4 tbsp golden (light corn) syrup

400 g/14 oz canned condensed milk

A few drops of vanilla essence (extract)

For the topping:
225 g/8 oz/2 cups plain (semi-sweet) chocolate

To make the base, rub the butter or margarine into the flour, then stir in the sugar and knead the mixture to a firm dough. Press into the base of a greased Swiss roll tin (jelly roll pan) lined with foil. Bake in a preheated oven at 180°C/ 350°F/gas mark 4 for 35 minutes until golden. Leave in the tin to cool.

To make the filling, melt the butter or margarine, sugar, syrup and condensed milk in a pan over a low heat, stirring continuously. Bring to the boil, then simmer gently, stirring continuously, for 7 minutes. Remove from the heat, add the vanilla essence and beat thoroughly. Pour over the base and leave to cool and set.

Melt the chocolate in a heatproof bowl set over a pan of gently simmering water. Spread over the caramel layer and mark into patterns with a fork. Leave to cool and set, then cut into squares.

Wholemeal Oat Shortbread

Makes 10

100 g/4 oz/½ cup butter or margarine

150 g/5 oz/1¼ cups wholemeal (wholewheat) flour

25 g/1 oz/¼ cup oat flour

50 g/2 oz/¼ cup soft brown sugar

Rub the butter or margarine into the flours until the mixture resembles breadcrumbs. Stir in the sugar and lightly work to a soft, crumbly dough. Roll out on a lightly floured surface to about 1 cm/½ in thick and cut into 5 cm/2 in rounds with a biscuit (cookie) cutter. Transfer carefully to a greased baking (cookie) sheet and bake in a preheated oven at 150°C/300°F/gas mark 3 for about 40 minutes until golden and firm.

Almond Whirls

Makes 16

175 g/6 oz/¾ cup butter or margarine, softened

50 g/2 oz/1/3 cup icing (confectioners') sugar, sifted

2.5 ml/½ tsp almond essence (extract)

175 g/6 oz/1½ cups plain (all-purpose) flour

8 glacé (candied) cherries, halved or quartered

Icing (confectioners') sugar, sifted, for dusting

Cream together the butter or margarine and sugar. Beat in the almond essence and flour. Transfer the mixture to a piping bag fitted with a large star-shaped nozzle (tip). Pipe 16 flat whirls on to a greased baking (cookie) sheet. Top each one with a piece of cherry. Bake in a preheated oven at 160°C/325°F/gas mark 3 for 20 minutes until pale golden. Leave on the tray to cool for 5 minutes then transfer to a wire rack and dust with icing sugar.

Chocolate Meringue Shortbread

Makes 24

100 g/4 oz/½ cup butter or margarine, softened

5 ml/1 tsp vanilla essence (extract)

4 egg whites

200 g/7 oz/1¾ cups plain (all-purpose) flour

50 g/2 oz/¼ cup caster (superfine) sugar

45 ml/3 tbsp cocoa (unsweetened chocolate) powder

100 g/4 oz/2/3 cup icing (confectioners') sugar, sifted

Beat together the butter or margarine, vanilla essence and two of the egg whites. Mix together the flour, sugar and cocoa, then gradually beat into the butter mixture. Press into a greased 30 cm/12 in square tin (pan). Beat together the remaining egg whites with the icing sugar and spread over the top. Bake in a preheated oven at 190°C/375°F/gas mark 5 for 20 minutes until golden brown. Cut into bars.

Biscuit People

Makes about 12

100 g/4 oz/½ cup butter or margarine, softened

100 g/4 oz/½ cup caster (superfine) sugar

1 egg, beaten

225 g/8 oz/2 cups plain (all-purpose) flour

A few currants and glacé (candied) cherries

Cream together the butter or margarine and sugar. Gradually add the egg and beat thoroughly. Fold in the flour using a metal spoon. Roll out the mixture on a lightly floured surface to about 5 mm/¼ in thick. Cut out people with a biscuit (cookie) cutter or knife, re-rolling the trimmings until you have used all the dough. Place on a greased baking (cookie) sheet and press in currants for eyes and buttons. Cut slices of cherry for the mouths. Bake the biscuits (cookies) in a preheated oven at 190°C/375°F/gas mark 5 for 10 minutes until pale brown. Leave to cool on a wire rack.

Iced Ginger Shortcake

Makes two 20 cm/8 in cakes

For the shortcake:

225 g/8 oz/1 cup butter or margarine, softened

100 g/4 oz/½ cup caster (superfine) sugar

275 g/10 oz/2½ cups plain (all-purpose) flour

10 ml/2 tsp baking powder

10 ml/2 tsp ground ginger

For the icing (frosting):

50 g/2 oz/¼ cup butter or margarine

15 ml/1 tbsp golden (light corn) syrup

100 g/4 oz/2/3 cup icing (confectioners') sugar, sifted

5 ml/1 tsp ground ginger

To make the shortcake, cream together the butter or margarine and sugar until light and fluffy. Mix in the remaining shortcake ingredients to make a dough, divide the mixture in half and press into two greased 20 cm/8 in sandwich tins (pans). Bake in a preheated oven at 160°C/325°F/gasmark 3 for 40 minutes.

To make the icing, melt the butter or margarine and syrup in a pan. Add the icing sugar and ginger and blend together well. Pour over both shortcakes and leave until cool, then cut into wedges.

Shrewsbury Biscuits

Makes 24

100 g/4 oz/½ cup butter or margarine, softened

100 g/4 oz/½ cup caster (superfine) sugar

1 egg yolk

225 g/8 oz/2 cups plain (all-purpose) flour

5 ml/1 tsp baking powder

5 ml/1 tsp grated lemon rind

Cream together the butter or margarine and sugar until light and fluffy. Gradually beat in the egg yolk, then work in the flour, baking powder and lemon rind, finishing with your hands until the mixture binds together. Roll out to 5 mm/ ¼ in thick and cut into 6 cm/2¼ in rounds with a biscuit (cookie) cutter. Place the biscuits well apart on a greased baking (cookie) sheet and prick them with a fork. Bake in a preheated oven at 180°C/350°F/ gas mark 4 for 15 minutes until pale golden.

Spanish Spiced Biscuits

Makes 16

90 ml/6 tbsp olive oil

100 g/4 oz/½ cup granulated sugar

100 g/4 oz/1 cup plain (all-purpose) flour

15 ml/1 tbsp baking powder

10 ml/2 tsp ground cinnamon

3 eggs

Grated rind of 1 lemon

30 ml/2 tbsp icing (confectioners') sugar, sifted

Warm the oil in a small pan. Mix together the sugar, flour, baking powder and cinnamon. In a separate bowl, beat the eggs and lemon rind until frothy. Stir in the dry ingredients and oil to make a smooth batter. Pour the batter into a well-greased Swiss roll tin (jelly roll pan) and bake in a preheated oven at 180°C/350°F/gas mark 4 for 30 minutes until golden. Turn out, leave to cool, then cut into triangles and sprinkle the biscuits (cookies) with icing sugar.

Old-fashioned Spice Biscuits

Makes 24

75 g/3 oz/1/3 cup butter or margarine

50 g/2 oz/¼ cup caster (superfine) sugar

45 ml/3 tbsp black treacle (molasses)

175 g/6 oz/¾ cup plain (all-purpose) flour

5 ml/1 tsp ground cinnamon

5 ml/1 tsp ground mixed (apple-pie) spice

2.5 ml/½ tsp ground ginger

2.5 ml/½ tsp bicarbonate of soda (baking soda)

Melt the butter or margarine, sugar and treacle together over a low heat. Mix together the flour, spices and bicarbonate of soda in a bowl. Pour into the treacle mixture and mix together until well blended. Blend to a soft dough and shape into small balls. Arrange, well apart, on a greased baking (cookie) sheet and press flat with a fork. Bake the biscuits (cookies) in a preheated oven at 180°C/350°F/gas mark 4 for 12 minutes until firm and golden.

Treacle Biscuits

Makes 24

75 g/3 oz/1/3 cup butter or margarine, softened

100 g/4 oz/½ cup soft brown sugar

1 egg yolk

30 ml/2 tbsp black treacle (molasses)

100 g/4 oz/1 cup plain (all-purpose) flour

5 ml/1 tsp bicarbonate of soda (baking soda)

A pinch of salt

5 ml/1 tsp ground cinnamon

2.5 ml/½ tsp ground cloves

Beat together the butter or margarine and sugar until light and fluffy. Gradually beat in the egg yolk and molasses. Mix together the flour, bicarbonate of soda, salt and spices and blend into the mixture. Cover and chill.

Roll the mixture into 3 cm/1½ in balls and arrange on a greased baking (cookie) sheet. Bake the biscuits (cookies) in a preheated oven at 180°C/350°F/gas mark 4 for 10 minutes until just set.

Treacle, Apricot and Nut Cookies

Makes about 24

50 g/2 oz/¼ cup butter or margarine

50 g/2 oz/¼ cup caster (superfine) sugar

50 g/2 oz/¼ cup soft brown sugar

1 egg, lightly beaten

2.5 ml/½ tsp bicarbonate of soda (baking soda)

30 ml/2 tbsp warm water

45 ml/3 tbsp black treacle (molasses)

25 g/1 oz ready-to-eat dried apricots, chopped

25 g/1 oz/¼ cup chopped mixed nuts

100 g/4 oz/1 cup plain (all-purpose) flour

A pinch of salt

A pinch of ground cloves

Cream together the butter or margarine and sugars until light and fluffy. Gradually beat in the egg. Mix the bicarbonate of soda with the water, the stir into the mixture with the remaining ingredients. Drop spoonfuls on to a greased baking (cookie) sheet and bake in a preheated oven at 180°C/350°F/gas mark 4 for 10 minutes.

Treacle and Buttermilk Cookies

Makes 24

50 g/2 oz/¼ cup butter or margarine, softened

50 g/2 oz/¼ cup soft brown sugar

150 ml/¼ pt/2/3 cup black treacle (molasses)

150 ml/¼ pt/2/3 cup buttermilk

175 g/6 oz/1½ cups plain (all-purpose) flour

2.5 ml/½ tsp bicarbonate of soda (baking soda)

Cream together the butter or margarine and sugar until light and fluffy, then mix in the treacle and buttermilk alternately with the flour and bicarbonate of soda. Drop large spoonfuls on to a greased baking (cookie) sheet and bake in a preheated oven at 190°C/375°F/ gas mark 5 for 10 minutes.

Treacle and Coffee Biscuits

Makes 24

60 g/2½ oz/1/3 cup lard (shortening)

50 g/2 oz/¼ cup soft brown sugar

75 g/3 oz/¼ cup black treacle (molasses)

2.5 ml/½ tsp vanilla essence (extract)

200 g/7 oz/1¾ cups plain (all-purpose) flour

5 ml/1 tsp bicarbonate of soda (baking soda)

A pinch of salt

2.5 ml/½ tsp ground ginger

2.5 ml/½ tsp ground cinnamon

60 ml/4 tbsp cold black coffee

Cream together the lard and sugar until light and fluffy. Stir in the treacle and vanilla essence. Mix together the flour, bicarbonate of soda, salt and spices and beat into the mixture alternately with the coffee. Cover and chill for several hours.

Roll out the dough to 5 mm/¼ in thick and cut into 5 cm/2 in rounds with a biscuit (cookie) cutter. Place the biscuits on an ungreased baking (cookie) sheet and bake in a preheated oven at 190°C/375°F/gas mark 5 for 10 minutes until firm to the touch.

Treacle and Date Cookies

Makes about 24

50 g/2 oz/¼ cup butter or margarine, softened

50 g/2 oz/¼ cup caster (superfine) sugar

50 g/2 oz/¼ cup soft brown sugar

1 egg, lightly beaten

2.5 ml/½ tsp bicarbonate of soda (baking soda)

30 ml/2 tbsp warm water

45 ml/3 tbsp black treacle (molasses)

25 g/1 oz/¼ cup stoned (pitted) dates, chopped

100 g/4 oz/1 cup plain (all-purpose) flour

A pinch of salt

A pinch of ground cloves

Cream together the butter or margarine and sugars until light and fluffy. Gradually beat in the egg. Mix the bicarbonate of soda with the water, then stir into the mixture with the remaining ingredients. Drop spoonfuls on to a greased baking (cookie) sheet and bake in a preheated oven at 180°C/350°F/gas mark 4 for 10 minutes.

Treacle and Ginger Cookies

Makes 24

50 g/2 oz/¼ cup butter or margarine, softened

50 g/2 oz/¼ cup soft brown sugar

150 ml/¼ pt/2/3 cup black treacle (molasses)

150 ml/¼ pt/2/3 cup buttermilk

175 g/6 oz/1½ cups plain (all-purpose) flour

2.5 ml/½ tsp bicarbonate of soda (baking soda)

2.5 ml/½ tsp ground ginger

1 egg, beaten, to glaze

Cream together the butter or margarine and sugar until light and fluffy, then mix in the treacle and buttermilk alternately with the flour, bicarbonate of soda and ground ginger. Drop large spoonfuls on to a greased baking (cookie) sheet and brush the tops with beaten egg. Bake in a preheated oven at 190°C/375°F/ gas mark 5 for 10 minutes.

Vanilla Biscuits

Makes 24

150 g/5 oz/2/3 cup butter or margarine, softened

100 g/4 oz/½ cup caster (superfine) sugar

1 egg, beaten

225 g/8 oz/2 cups self-raising (self-rising) flour

A pinch of salt

10 ml/2 tsp vanilla essence (extract)

Glacé (candied) cherries to decorate

Cream together the butter or margarine and sugar until light and fluffy. Gradually beat in the egg, then fold in the flour, salt and vanilla essence and mix to a dough. Knead until smooth. Wrap in clingfim (plastic wrap) and chill for 20 minutes.

Roll out the dough thinly and cut into rounds with a biscuit (cookie) cutter. Arrange on a greased baking (cookie) sheet and place a cherry on top of each one. Bake the biscuits in a preheated oven at 180°C/350°F/gas mark 4 for 10 minutes until golden brown. Leave to cool on the baking sheet for 10 minutes before transferring to a wire rack to finish cooling.

Walnut Biscuits

Makes 36

100 g/4 oz/½ cup butter or margarine, softened

100 g/4 oz/½ cup soft brown sugar

100 g/4 oz/½ cup caster (superfine) sugar

1 large egg, lightly beaten

200 g/7 oz/1¾ cups plain (all-purpose) flour

5 ml/1 tsp baking powder

2.5 ml/½ tsp bicarbonate of soda (baking soda)

120 ml/4 fl oz/½ cup buttermilk

50 g/2 oz/½ cup walnuts, chopped

Cream together the butter or margarine and sugars. Gradually beat in the egg, then fold in the flour, baking powder and bicarbonate of soda alternately with the buttermilk. Fold in the walnuts. Drop small spoonfuls on to a greased baking (cookie) sheet and bake the biscuits (cookies) in a preheated oven at 190°C/375°F/gas mark 5 for 10 minutes.

Crisp Biscuits

Makes 24

25 g/1 oz fresh yeast or 40 ml/ 2½ tbsp dried yeast

450 ml/¾ pt/2 cups warm milk

900 g/2 lb/8 cups strong plain (bread) flour

175 g/6 oz/¾ cup butter or margarine, softened

30 ml/2 tbsp clear honey

2 eggs, beaten

Beaten egg for glazing

Mix the yeast with a little of the warm milk and leave in a warm place for 20 minutes. Place the flour in a bowl and rub in the butter or margarine. Blend in the yeast mixture, the remaining warm milk, the honey and eggs and mix to a soft dough. Knead on a lightly floured surface until smooth and elastic. Place in an oiled bowl, cover with oiled clingfilm (plastic wrap) and leave in a warm place for 1 hour until doubled in size.

Knead again, then shape into long flat rolls and place on a greased baking (cookie) sheet. Cover with oiled clingfilm and leave in a warm place for 20 minutes.

Brush with beaten egg and bake in a preheated oven at 200°C/400°F/gas mark 6 for 20 minutes. Leave to cool overnight.

Slice thinly, then bake again in a preheated oven at 150°C/300°F/gas mark 2 for 30 minutes until crisp and brown.

Cheddar Biscuits

Makes 12

50 g/2 oz/¼ cup butter or margarine

200 g/7 oz/1¾ cups plain (all-purpose) flour

15 ml/1 tbsp baking powder

A pinch of salt

50 g/2 oz/½ cup Cheddar cheese, grated

175 ml/6 fl oz/¾ cup milk

Rub the butter or margarine into the flour, baking powder and salt until the mixture resembles breadcrumbs. Stir in the cheese, then mix in enough of the milk to make a soft dough. Roll out on a lightly floured surface to about 2 cm/ ¾ in thick and cut into rounds with a biscuit (cookie) cutter. Arrange on an ungreased baking (cookie) sheet and bake the biscuits (crackers) in a preheated oven at 200°C/400°F/gas mark 6 for 15 minutes until golden brown.

Blue Cheese Biscuits

Makes 12

50 g/2 oz/¼ cup butter or margarine

200 g/7 oz/1¾ cups plain (all-purpose) flour

15 ml/1 tbsp baking powder

50 g/2 oz/½ cup Stilton cheese, grated or crumbled

175 ml/6 fl oz/¾ cup milk

Rub the butter or margarine into the flour and baking powder until the mixture resembles breadcrumbs. Stir in the cheese, then mix in enough of the milk to make a soft dough. Roll out on a lightly floured surface to about 2 cm/ ¾ in thick and cut into rounds with a biscuit (cookie) cutter. Arrange on an ungreased baking (cookie) sheet and bake the biscuits (crackers) in a preheated oven at 200°C/400°F/gas mark 6 for 15 minutes until golden brown.

Cheese and Sesame Biscuits

Makes 24

75 g/3 oz/1/3 cup butter or margarine

75 g/3 oz/¾ cup wholemeal (wholewheat) flour

75 g/3 oz/¾ cup Cheddar cheese, grated

30 ml/2 tbsp sesame seeds

Salt and freshly ground black pepper

1 egg, beaten

Rub the butter or margarine into the flour until the mixture resembles breadcrumbs. Stir in the cheese and half the sesame seeds and season with salt and pepper. Press together to form a firm dough. Roll out the dough on a lightly floured surface to about 5 mm/¼ in thick and cut into rounds with a biscuit (cookie) cutter. Place the biscuits (crackers) on a greased baking (cookie) sheet, brush with egg and sprinkle with the remaining sesame seeds. Bake in a preheated oven at 190°C/375°F/gas mark 5 for 10 minutes until golden.

Cheese Straws

Makes 16

225 g/8 oz Puff Pastry

1 egg, beaten

100 g/4 oz/1 cup Cheddar or strong cheese, grated

15 ml/1 tbsp grated Parmesan cheese

Salt and freshly ground black pepper

Roll out the pastry (paste) to about 5 mm/¼ in thick and brush generously with beaten egg. Sprinkle with the cheeses and season to taste with salt and pepper. Cut into strips and twist the strips gently into spirals. Place on a dampened baking (cookie) sheet and bake in a preheated oven at 220°C/425°F/gas mark 7 for about 10 minutes until puffed and golden.

Cheese and Tomato Biscuits

Makes 12

50 g/2 oz/¼ cup butter or margarine

200 g/7 oz/1¾ cups plain (all-purpose) flour

15 ml/1 tbsp baking powder

A pinch of salt

50 g/2 oz/½ cup Cheddar cheese, grated

15 ml/1 tbsp tomato purée (paste)

150 ml/¼ pt/2/3 cup milk

Rub the butter or margarine into the flour, baking powder and salt until the mixture resembles breadcrumbs. Stir in the cheese, then mix in the tomato purée and enough of the milk to make a soft dough. Roll out on a lightly floured surface to about 2 cm/¾ in thick and cut into rounds with a biscuit (cookie) cutter. Arrange on an ungreased baking (cookie) sheet and bake the biscuits (crackers) in a preheated oven at 200°C/400°F/gas mark 6 for 15 minutes until golden brown.

Goats' Cheese Bites

Makes 30

2 sheets frozen filo pastry (paste), thawed

50 g/2 oz/¼ cup unsalted butter, melted

50 g/2 oz/½ cup goats' cheese, diced

5 ml/1 tsp Herbes de Provence

Brush a filo pastry sheet with melted butter, place the second sheet on top and brush with butter. Cut into 30 equal squares, place a piece of cheese on each one and sprinkle with herbs. Bring the corners together and twist to seal, then brush again with melted butter. Place on a greased baking (cookie) sheet and bake in a preheated oven at 180°C/350°F/gas mark 4 for 10 minutes until crisp and golden.

Ham and Mustard Rolls

Makes 16

225 g/8 oz Puff Pastry

30 ml/2 tbsp French mustard

100 g/4 oz/1 cup cooked ham, chopped

Salt and freshly ground black pepper

Roll out the pastry (paste) to about 5 mm/¼ in thick. Spread with the mustard, then sprinkle with the ham and season with salt and pepper. Roll up the pastry into a long sausage shape, then cut into 1 cm/½ in slices and arrange on a dampened baking (cookie) sheet. Bake in a preheated oven at 220°C/425°F/gas mark 7 for about 10 minutes until puffed and golden.

Ham and Pepper Biscuits

Makes 30

225 g/8 oz/2 cups plain (all-purpose) flour

15 ml/1 tbsp baking powder

5 ml/1 tsp dried thyme

5 ml/1 tsp caster (superfine) sugar

2.5 ml/½ tsp ground ginger

A pinch of grated nutmeg

A pinch of bicarbonate of soda (baking soda)

Salt and freshly ground black pepper

50 g/2 oz/¼ cup vegetable fat (shortening)

50 g/2 oz/½ cup cooked ham, minced

30 ml/2 tbsp finely chopped green (bell) pepper

175 ml/6 fl oz/¾ cup buttermilk

Mix together the flour, baking powder, thyme, sugar, ginger, nutmeg, bicarbonate of soda, salt and pepper. Rub in the vegetable fat until the mixture resembles breadcrumbs. Stir in the ham and pepper. Gradually add the buttermilk and mix to a soft dough. Knead for a few seconds on a lightly floured surface until smooth. Roll out to 2 cm/¾ in thick and cut into rounds with a biscuit (cookie) cutter. Place the biscuits, well apart, on a greased baking (cookie) sheet and bake in a preheated oven at 220°C/425°F/gas mark 7 for 12 minutes until puffed and golden.

Simple Herb Biscuits

Makes 8

225 g/8 oz/2 cups plain (all-purpose) flour

15 ml/1 tbsp baking powder

5 ml/1 tsp caster (superfine) sugar

2.5 ml/½ tsp salt

50 g/2 oz/¼ cup butter or margarine

15 ml/1 tbsp snipped fresh chives

A pinch of paprika

Freshly ground black pepper

45 ml/3 tbsp milk

45 ml/3 tbsp water

Mix together the flour, baking powder, sugar and salt. Rub in the butter or margarine until the mixture resembles breadcrumbs. Mix in the chives, paprika and pepper to taste. Stir in the milk and water and mix to a soft dough. Knead on a lightly floured surface until smooth, then roll out to 2 cm/¾ in thick and cut into rounds with a biscuit (cookie) cutter. Place the biscuits (crackers), well apart, on a greased baking (cookie) sheet and bake in a preheated oven at 200°C/400°F/gas mark 6 for 15 minutes until puffed and golden.

Indian Biscuits

Serves 4

100 g/4 oz/1 cup plain (all-purpose) flour

100 g/4 oz/1 cup semolina (cream of wheat)

175 g/6 oz/¾ cup caster (superfine) sugar

75 g/3 oz/¾ cup gram flour

175 g/6 oz/¾ cup ghee

Mix together all the ingredients in a bowl, then rub them with the palms of your hands to form a stiff dough. You may need a little more ghee if the mixture is too dry. Shape into small balls and press into biscuit (cracker) shapes. Place on a greased and lined baking (cookie) sheet and bake in a preheated oven at 150°C/ 300°F/gas mark 2 for 30–40 minutes until lightly browned. Fine hairline cracks may appear as the biscuits are cooked.

Hazelnut and Shallot Shortbread

Makes 12

75 g/3 oz/1/3 cup butter or margarine, softened

175 g/6 oz/1½ cups wholemeal (wholewheat) flour

10 ml/2 tsp baking powder

1 shallot, finely chopped

50 g/2 oz/½ cup hazelnuts, chopped

10 ml/2 tsp paprika

15 ml/1 tbsp cold water

Rub the butter or margarine into the flour and baking powder until the mixture resembles breadcrumbs. Stir in the shallot, hazelnuts and paprika. Add the cold water and press together to make a dough. Roll out and press into a 30 x 20 cm/12 x 8 in Swiss roll tin (jelly roll pan) and prick all over with a fork. Mark into fingers. Bake in a preheated oven at 200°C/400°F/gas mark 6 for 10 minutes until golden.

Salmon and Dill Biscuits

Makes 12

225 g/8 oz/2 cups plain (all-purpose) flour

5 ml/1 tsp caster (superfine) sugar

2.5 ml/½ tsp salt

20 ml/4 tsp baking powder

100 g/4 oz/½ cup butter or margarine, diced

90 ml/6 tbsp water

90 ml/6 tbsp milk

100 g/4 oz/1 cup smoked salmon trimmings, diced

60 ml/4 tbsp chopped fresh dill (dill weed)

Mix together the flour, sugar, salt and baking powder, then rub in the butter or margarine until the mixture resembles breadcrumbs. Gradually mix in the milk and water and mix to a soft dough. Work in the salmon and dill and mix until smooth. Roll out to 2.5 cm/1 in thick and cut into rounds with a biscuit (cookie) cutter. Place the biscuits (crackers) well apart on a greased baking (cookie) sheet and bake in a preheated oven at 220°C/425°F/gas mark 7 for 15 minutes until puffed and golden.

Soda Biscuits

Makes 12

45 ml/3 tbsp lard (shortening)

225 g/8 oz/2 cups plain (all-purpose) flour

5 ml/1 tsp bicarbonate of soda (baking soda)

5 ml/1 tsp cream of tartar

A pinch of salt

250 ml/8 fl oz/1 cup buttermilk

Rub the lard into the flour, bicarbonate of soda, cream of tartar and salt until the mixture resembles breadcrumbs. Stir in the milk and mix to a soft dough. Roll out on a lightly floured surface to 1 cm/½ in thick and cut out with a biscuit (cookie) cutter. Place the biscuits (crackers) on a greased baking (cookie) sheet and bake in a preheated oven at 230°C/450°F/gas mark 8 for 10 minutes until golden.

Tomato and Parmesan Pinwheels

Makes 16

225 g/8 oz Puff Pastry

30 ml/2 tbsp tomato purée (paste)

100 g/4 oz/1 cup Parmesan cheese, grated

Salt and freshly ground black pepper

Roll out the pastry (paste) to about 5 mm/¼ in thick. Spread with the tomato purée, then sprinkle with the cheese and season with salt and pepper. Roll up the pastry into a long sausage shape, then cut into 1 cm/½ in slices and arrange on a dampened baking (cookie) sheet. Bake in a preheated oven at 220°C/ 425°F/gas mark 7 for about 10 minutes until puffed and golden.

Tomato and Herb Biscuits

Makes 12

225 g/8 oz/2 cups plain (all-purpose) flour

5 ml/1 tsp caster (superfine) sugar

2.5 ml/½ tsp salt

40 ml/2½ tbsp baking powder

100 g/4 oz/½ cup butter or margarine

30 ml/2 tbsp milk

30 ml/2 tbsp water

4 ripe tomatoes, skinned, seeded and chopped

45 ml/3 tbsp chopped fresh basil

Mix together the flour, sugar, salt and baking powder. Rub in the butter or margarine until the mixture resembles breadcrumbs. Stir in the milk, water, tomatoes and basil and mix to a soft dough. Knead for a few seconds on a lightly floured surface, then roll out to 2.5 cm/1 in thick and cut into rounds with a biscuit (cookie) cutter. Place the biscuits well apart on a greased baking (cookie) sheet and bake in a preheated oven at 230°C/425°F/gas mark 7 for 15 minutes until puffed and golden.

Basic White Loaf

Makes three 450 g/1 lb loaves

25 g/1 oz fresh yeast or 40 ml/2½ tbsp dried yeast

10 ml/2 tsp sugar

900 ml/1½ pts/3¾ cups warm water

25 g/1 oz/2 tbsp lard (shortening)

1.5 kg/3 lb/12 cups strong plain (bread) flour

15 ml/1 tbsp salt

Blend the yeast with the sugar and a little of the warm water and leave in a warm place for 20 minutes until frothy. Rub the lard into the flour and salt, then stir in the yeast mixture and enough of the remaining water to mix to a firm dough that leaves the sides of the bowl cleanly. Knead on a lightly floured surface or in a processor until elastic and no longer sticky. Place the dough in an oiled bowl, cover with oiled clingfilm (plastic wrap) and leave in a warm place for about 1 hour until doubled in size and springy to the touch.

Knead the dough again until firm, divide into three and place in greased 450 g/1 lb loaf tins (pans) or shape into the loaves of your choice. Cover and leave to rise in a warm place for about 40 minutes until the dough reaches just above the top of the tins.

Bake in a preheated oven at 230°C/ 450°F/gas mark 8 for 30 minutes until the loaves begin to shrink away from the sides of the tins and are golden and firm, and hollow-sounding when tapped on the base.

Bagels

Makes 12

15 g/½ oz fresh yeast or 20 ml/ 4 tsp dried yeast

5 ml/1 tsp caster (superfine) sugar

300 ml/½ pt/1¼ cups warm milk

50 g/2 oz/¼ cup butter or margarine

450 g/1 lb/4 cups strong plain (bread) flour

A pinch of salt

1 egg yolk

30 ml/2 tbsp poppy seeds

Blend the yeast with the sugar and a little of the warm milk and leave in a warm place for 20 minutes until frothy. Rub the butter or margarine into the flour and salt and make a well in the centre. Add the yeast mixture, the remaining warm milk and the egg yolk and mix to a smooth dough. Knead until the dough is elastic and no longer sticky. Place in an oiled bowl, cover with oiled clingfilm (plastic wrap) and leave in a warm place for about 1 hour until doubled in size.

Knead the dough lightly, then cut it into 12 pieces. Roll each one into a long strip about 15 cm/6 in long and twist into a ring. Place on a greased baking (cookie) sheet, cover and leave to rise for 15 minutes.

Bring a large pan of water to the boil, then turn down the heat to a simmer. Drop a ring into the simmering water and cook for 3 minutes, turning once, then remove and place on a baking (cookie) sheet. Continue with the remaining bagels. Sprinkle the bagels with poppy seeds and bake in a preheated oven at 230°C/450°F/gas mark 8 for 20 minutes until golden.

Baps

Makes 12

25 g/1 oz fresh yeast or 40 ml/ 2½ tbsp dried yeast

5 ml/1 tsp caster (superfine) sugar

150 ml/¼ pt/2/3 cup warm milk

50 g/2 oz/¼ cup lard (shortening)

450 g/1 lb/4 cups strong plain (bread) flour

5 ml/1 tsp salt

150 ml/¼ pt/2/3 cup warm water

Blend the yeast with the sugar and a little of the warm milk and leave in a warm place for 20 minutes until frothy. Rub the lard into the flour, then stir in the salt and make a well in the centre. Add the yeast mixture, the remaining milk and the water and mix to a soft dough. Knead until elastic and no longer sticky. Place in an oiled bowl and cover with oiled clingfilm (plastic wrap). Leave in a warm place for about 1 hour until doubled in size.

Shape the dough into 12 flat rolls and arrange on a greased baking (cookie) sheet. Leave to rise for 15 minutes.

Bake in a preheated oven at 230°C/ 450°F/gas mark 8 for 15–20 minutes until well risen and golden.

Creamy Barley Loaf

Makes one 900 g/2 lb loaf

15 g/½ oz fresh yeast or 20 ml/4 tsp dried yeast

A pinch of sugar

350 ml/12 fl oz/1½ cups warm water

400 g/14 oz/3½ cups strong plain (bread) flour

175 g/6 oz/1½ cups barley flour

A pinch of salt

45 ml/3 tbsp single (light) cream

Blend the yeast with the sugar and a little of the warm water and leave in a warm place for 20 minutes until frothy. Mix the flours and salt in a bowl, add the yeast mixture, the cream and remaining water and mix to a firm dough. Knead until smooth and no longer sticky. Place in an oiled bowl, cover with oiled clingfilm (plastic wrap) and leave in a warm place for about 1 hour until doubled in size.

Knead again lightly, then shape into a greased 900 g/2 lb loaf tin (pan), cover and leave in a warm place for 40 minutes until the dough has risen above the top of the tin.

Bake in a preheated oven at 220°C/ 425°F/gas mark 7 for 10 minutes, then reduce the oven temperature to 190°C/375°F/gas mark 5 and bake for a further 25 minutes until golden brown and hollow-sounding when tapped on the base.

Beer Bread

Makes one 900 g/2 lb loaf

450 g/1 lb/4 cups self-raising (self-rising) flour

5 ml/1 tsp salt

350 ml/12 fl oz/1½ cups lager

Mix together the ingredients to a smooth dough. Shape into a greased 900 g/2 lb loaf tin (pan), cover and leave to rise in a warm place for 20 minutes. Bake in a preheated oven at 190°C/375°F/gas mark 5 for 45 minutes until golden brown and hollow-sounding when tapped on the base.

Boston Brown Bread

Makes three 450 g/1 lb loaves

100 g/4 oz/1 cup rye flour

100 g/4 oz/1 cup cornmeal

100 g/4 oz/1 cup wholemeal (wholewheat) flour

5 ml/1 tsp bicarbonate of soda (baking soda)

5 ml/1 tsp salt

250 g/9 oz/¾ cup black treacle (molasses)

500 ml/16 fl oz/2 cups buttermilk

175 g/6 oz/1 cup raisins

Mix together the dry ingredients, then stir in the treacle, buttermilk and raisins and mix to a soft dough. Spoon the mixture into three greased 450 g/1 lb pudding basins, cover with greaseproof (waxed) paper and foil and tie with string to seal the tops. Place in a large pan and fill with enough hot water to come half- way up the sides of the bowls. Bring the water to the boil, cover the pan and simmer for 2½ hours, topping up with boiling water as necessary. Remove the bowls from the pan and leave to cool slightly. Serve warm with butter.

Bran Flowerpots

Makes 3

25 g/1 oz fresh yeast or 40 ml/ 2½ tbsp dried yeast

5 ml/1 tsp sugar

600 ml/1 pt/2½ cups lukewarm water

675 g/1½ lb/6 cups wholemeal (wholewheat) flour

25 g/1 oz/¼ cup soya flour

5 ml/1 tsp salt

50 g/2 oz/1 cup bran

Milk to glaze

45 ml/3 tbsp cracked wheat

You will need three clean, new 13 cm/ 5 in clay flowerpots. Grease them well and bake in a hot oven for 30 minutes to prevent them from cracking.

Blend the yeast with the sugar and a little of the warm water and leave to stand until frothy. Mix the flours, salt and bran and make a well in the centre. Mix in the warm water and yeast mixture and knead to a firm dough. Turn out on to a floured surface and knead for about 10 minutes until smooth and elastic. Alternatively, you can do this in a food processor. Place the dough in a clean bowl, cover with oiled clingfilm (plastic wrap) and leave in a warm place to rise for about 1 hour until doubled in size.

Turn out on to a floured surface and knead again for 10 minutes. Shape into the three greased flowerpots, cover and leave to prove for 45 minutes until the dough has risen above the top of the pots.

Brush the dough with milk and sprinkle with the cracked wheat. Bake in a preheated oven at 230°C/450°F/gas mark 8 for 15 minutes. Reduce the oven temperature to 200°C/400°F/gas mark 6 and bake for a further 30 minutes until well risen and firm. Turn out and leave to cool.

Buttered Rolls

Makes 12

450 g/1 lb Basic White Loaf dough

100 g/4 oz/½ cup butter or margarine, diced

Make the bread dough and leave it to rise until doubled in size and springy to the touch.

Knead the dough again and work in the butter or margarine. Shape into 12 rolls and place them well apart on a greased baking (cookie) sheet. Cover with oiled clingfilm (plastic wrap) and leave to rise in a warm place for about 1 hour until doubled in size.

Bake in a preheated oven at 230°C/ 450°F/gas mark 8 for 20 minutes until golden brown and hollow-sounding when tapped on the base.

Buttermilk Loaf

Makes one 675 g/1½ lb loaf

450 g/1 lb/4 cups plain (all-purpose) flour

5 ml/1 tsp cream of tartar

5 ml/1 tsp bicarbonate of soda (baking soda)

250 ml/8 fl oz/1 cup buttermilk

Mix together the flour, cream of tartar and bicarbonate of soda in a bowl and make a well in the centre. Stir in enough of the buttermilk to mix to a soft dough. Shape into a round and place on a greased baking (cookie) sheet. Bake in a preheated oven at 220°C/425°F/gas mark 7 for 20 minutes until well risen and golden brown.

Canadian Corn Bread

Makes one 23 cm/9 in loaf

150 g/5 oz/1¼ cups plain (all-purpose) flour

75 g/3 oz/¾ cup cornmeal

15 ml/1 tbsp baking powder

2.5 ml/½ tsp salt

100 g/4 oz/1/3 cup maple syrup

100 g/4 oz/½ cup lard (shortening), melted

2 eggs, beaten

Mix together the dry ingredients, then blend in the syrup, lard and eggs and stir until well mixed. Spoon into a greased 23 cm/9 in baking tin (pan) and bake in a preheated oven at 220°C/425°F/ gas mark 7 for 25 minutes until well risen and golden brown, and beginning to shrink away from the sides of the tin.

Cornish Rolls

Makes 12

25 g/1 oz fresh yeast or 40 ml/2½ tbsp dried yeast

15 ml/1 tbsp caster (superfine) sugar

300 ml/½ pt/1¼ cups warm milk

50 g/2 oz/¼ cup butter or margarine

450 g/1 lb/4 cups strong plain (bread) flour

A pinch of salt

Blend the yeast with the sugar and a little of the warm milk and leave in a warm place for 20 minutes until frothy. Rub the butter or margarine into the flour and salt and make a well in the centre. Add the yeast mixture and the remaining milk and mix to a soft dough. Knead until elastic and no longer sticky. Place in an oiled bowl and cover with oiled clingfilm (plastic wrap). Leave in a warm place for about 1 hour until doubled in size.

Shape the dough into 12 flat rolls and arrange on a greased baking (cookie) sheet. Cover with oiled clingfilm and leave to rise for 15 minutes.

Bake in a preheated oven at 230°C/ 450°F/gas mark 8 for 15–20 minutes until well risen and golden.

Country Flat Bread

Makes six small breads

10 ml/2 tsp dried yeast

15 ml/1 tbsp clear honey

120 ml/4 fl oz/½ cup warm water

350 g/12 oz/3 cups strong plain (bread) flour

5 ml/1 tsp salt

50 g/2 oz/¼ cup butter or margarine

5 ml/1 tsp caraway seeds

5 ml/1 tsp ground coriander

5 ml/1 tsp ground cardamom

120 ml/4 fl oz/½ cup warm milk

60 ml/4 tbsp sesame seeds

Blend the yeast and honey with 45 ml/3 tbsp of the warm water and 15 ml/1 tbsp of the flour and leave for about 20 minutes in a warm place until frothy. Mix the remaining flour with the salt, then rub in the butter or margarine and stir in the caraway seeds, coriander and cardamom and make a well in the centre. Mix in the yeast mixture, the remaining water and enough of the milk to make a smooth dough. Knead well until firm and no longer sticky. Place in an oiled bowl, cover with oiled clingfilm (plastic wrap) and leave in a warm place for about 30 minutes until doubled in size.

Knead the dough again, then shape into flat cakes. Place on a greased baking (cookie) sheet and brush with milk. Sprinkle with sesame seeds. Cover with oiled clingfilm and leave to rise for 15 minutes.

Bake in a preheated oven at 200°C/ 400°F/gas mark 6 for 30 minutes until golden.

Country Poppyseed Plait

Makes one 450 g/1 lb loaf

275 g/10 oz/2½ cups plain (all-purpose) flour

25 g/1 oz/2 tbsp caster (superfine) sugar

5 ml/1 tsp salt

10 ml/2 tsp easy-blend dried yeast

175 ml/6 fl oz/¾ cup milk

25 g/1 oz/2 tbsp butter or margarine

1 egg

A little milk or egg white for glazing

30 ml/2 tbsp poppy seeds

Mix together the flour, sugar, salt and yeast. Warm the milk with the butter or margarine, then mix into the flour with the egg and knead to a stiff dough. Knead until elastic and no longer sticky. Place in an oiled bowl, cover with oiled clingfilm (plastic wrap) and leave in a warm place for about 1 hour until doubled in size.

Knead again and shape into three sausage shapes about 20 cm/8 in long. Moisten one end of each strip and press them together, then plait the strips together, moisten and seal the ends. Place on a greased baking (cookie) sheet, cover with oiled clingfilm and leave to rise for about 40 minutes until doubled in size.

Brush with milk or egg white and sprinkle with poppy seeds. Bake in a preheated oven at 190°C/375°F/gas mark 5 for about 45 minutes until golden brown.

Country Wholemeal Bread

Makes two 450 g/1 lb loaves

20 ml/4 tsp dried yeast

5 ml/1 tsp caster (superfine) sugar

600 ml/1 pt/2½ cups warm water

25 g/1 oz/2 tbsp vegetable fat (shortening)

800 g/1¾ lb/7 cups wholemeal (wholewheat) flour

10 ml/2 tsp salt

10 ml/2 tsp malt extract

1 egg, beaten

25 g/1 oz/¼ cup cracked wheat

Blend the yeast with the sugar and a little of the warm water and leave for about 20 minutes until frothy. Rub the fat into the flour, salt and malt extract and make a well in the centre. Stir in the yeast mixture and the remaining warm water and mix to a soft dough. Knead well until elastic and no longer sticky. Place in an oiled bowl, cover with oiled clingfilm (plastic wrap) and leave in a warm place for about 1 hour until doubled in size.

Knead the dough again and shape into two greased 450 g/1 lb loaf tins (pans). Leave to rise in a warm place for about 40 minutes until the dough rises just above the tops of the tins.

Brush the tops of the loaves generously with egg and sprinkle with cracked wheat. Bake in a preheated oven at 230°C/ 450°F/gas mark 8 for about 30 minutes until golden brown and hollow-sounding when tapped on the base.

Curry Plaits

Makes two 450 g/1 lb loaves

120 ml/4 fl oz/½ cup warm water

30 ml/2 tbsp dried yeast

225 g/8 oz/2/3 cup clear honey

25 g/1 oz/2 tbsp butter or margarine

30 ml/2 tbsp curry powder

675 g/1½ lb/6 cups plain (all-purpose) flour

10 ml/2 tsp salt

450 ml/¾ pt/2 cups buttermilk

1 egg

10 ml/2 tsp water

45 ml/3 tbsp flaked (slivered) almonds

Mix the water with the yeast and 5 ml/1 tsp of the honey and leave to stand for 20 minutes until frothy. Melt the butter or margarine, then stir in the curry powder and cook over a low heat for 1 minute. Stir in the remaining honey and remove from the heat. Place half the flour and the salt in a bowl and make a well in the centre. Add the yeast mixture, the honey mixture and the buttermilk and gradually add the remaining flour as you mix to a soft dough. Knead until smooth and elastic. Place in an oiled bowl, cover with oiled clingfilm and leave in a warm place for about 1 hour until doubled in size.

Knead again and divide the dough in half. Cut each piece into three and roll into 20 cm/8 in sausage shapes. Moisten one end of each strip and press together in two lots of three to seal. Plait the two sets of strips and seal the ends. Place on a greased baking (cookie) sheet, cover with oiled clingfilm (plastic wrap) and leave to rise for about 40 minutes until doubled in size.

Beat the egg with the water and brush over the loaves, then sprinkle with almonds. Bake in a preheated oven at 190°C/375°F/gas mark 5 for 40 minutes until golden brown and hollow-sounding when tapped on the base.

Devon Splits

Makes 12

25 g/1 oz fresh yeast or 40 ml/ 2½ tbsp dried yeast

5 ml/1 tsp caster (superfine) sugar

150 ml/¼ pt/2/3 cup warm milk

50 g/2 oz/¼ cup butter or margarine

450 g/1 lb/4 cups strong plain (bread) flour

150 ml/¼ pt/2/3 cup warm water

Blend the yeast with the sugar and a little warm milk and leave in a warm place for 20 minutes until frothy. Rub the butter or margarine into the flour and make a well in the centre. Add the yeast mixture, the remaining milk and the water and mix to a soft dough. Knead until elastic and no longer sticky. Place in an oiled bowl and cover with oiled clingfilm (plastic wrap). Leave in a warm place for about 1 hour until doubled in size.

Shape the dough into 12 flat rolls and arrange on a greased baking (cookie) sheet. Leave to rise for 15 minutes.

Bake in a preheated oven at 230°C/ 450°F/gas mark 8 for 15–20 minutes until well risen and golden brown.

Fruited Wheatgerm Bread

Makes one 900 g/2 lb loaf

225 g/8 oz/2 cups plain (all-purpose) flour

5 ml/1 tsp salt

5 ml/1 tsp bicarbonate of soda (baking soda)

5 ml/1 tsp baking powder

175 g/6 oz/1½ cups wheatgerm

100 g/4 oz/1 cup cornmeal

100 g/4 oz/1 cup rolled oats

350 g/12 oz/2 cups sultanas (golden raisins)

1 egg, lightly beaten

250 ml/8 fl oz/1 cup plain yoghurt

150 ml/¼ pt/2/3 cup black treacle (molasses)

60 ml/4 tbsp golden (light corn) syrup

30 ml/2 tbsp oil

Mix together the dry ingredients and the sultanas and make a well
in the centre. Blend together the egg, yoghurt, treacle, syrup and
oil, then stir into the dry ingredients and mix to a softish dough.
Shape into a greased 900 g/2 lb loaf tin (pan) and bake in a
preheated oven at 180°C/350°F/gas mark 4 for 1 hour until firm
to the touch. Leave to cool in the tin for 10 minutes before turning
out on to a wire rack to finish cooling.

Fruity Milk Plaits

Makes two 450 g/1 lb loaves

15 g/½ oz fresh yeast or 20 ml/ 4 tsp dried yeast

5 ml/1 tsp caster (superfine) sugar

450 ml/¾ pt/2 cups warm milk

50 g/2 oz/¼ cup butter or margarine

675 g/1½ lb/6 cups plain (all-purpose) flour

A pinch of salt

100 g/4 oz/2/3 cup raisins

25 g/1 oz/3 tbsp currants

25 g/1 oz/3 tbsp chopped mixed (candied) peel

Milk for glazing

Blend together the yeast with the sugar and a little of the warm milk. Leave to stand in a warm place for about 20 minutes until frothy. Rub the butter or margarine into the flour and salt, stir in the raisins, currants and mixed peel and make a well in the centre. Mix in the remaining warm milk and the yeast mixture and knead to a soft but not sticky dough. Place in an oiled bowl and cover with oiled clingfilm (plastic wrap). Leave in a warm place for about 1 hour until doubled in size.

Knead again lightly, then divide in half. Divide each half into three and roll into sausage shapes. Moisten one end of each roll and press three gently together, then plait the dough, moisten and seal the ends. Repeat with the other dough plait. Place on a greased baking (cookie) sheet, cover with oiled clingfilm (plastic wrap) and leave to rise for about 15 minutes.

Brush with a little milk, then bake in a preheated oven at 200°C/400°F/gas mark 6 for 30 minutes until golden brown and hollow-sounding when tapped on the base.

Granary Bread

Makes two 900 g/2 lb loaves

25 g/1 oz fresh yeast or 40 ml/ 2½ tbsp dried yeast

5 ml/1 tsp honey

450 ml/¾ pt/2 cups warm water

350 g/12 oz/3 cups granary flour

350 g/12 oz/3 cups wholemeal (wholewheat) flour

15 ml/1 tbsp salt

15 g/½ oz/1 tbsp butter or margarine

Blend the yeast with the honey and a little of the warm water and leave in a warm place for about 20 minutes until frothy. Mix the flours and salt and rub in the butter or margarine. Blend in the yeast mixture and enough of the warm water to make a smooth dough. Knead on a lightly floured surface until smooth and no longer sticky. Place in an oiled bowl, cover with oiled clingfilm (plastic wrap) and leave in a warm place for about 1 hour until doubled in size.

Knead again and shape into two greased 900 g/2 lb loaf tins (pans). Cover with oiled clingfilm and leave to rise until the dough reaches to the top of the tins.

Bake in a preheated oven at 220°C/ 425°F/gas mark 7 for 25 minutes until golden brown and hollow-sounding when tapped on the base.

Granary Rolls

Makes 12

15 g/½ oz fresh yeast or 20 ml/ 2½ tbsp dried yeast

5 ml/1 tsp caster (superfine) sugar

300 ml/½ pt/1¼ cups warm water

450 g/1 lb/4 cups granary flour

5 ml/1 tsp salt

5 ml/1 tbsp malt extract

30 ml/2 tbsp cracked wheat

Blend the yeast with the sugar and a little of the warm water and leave in a warm place until frothy. Mix together the flour and salt, then blend in the yeast mixture, the remaining warm water and the malt extract. Knead on a lightly floured surface until smooth and elastic. Place in an oiled bowl, cover with oiled clingfilm (plastic wrap) and leave in a warm place for about 1 hour until doubled in size.

Knead lightly, then shape into rolls and place on a greased baking (cookie) sheet. Brush with water and sprinkle with cracked wheat. Cover with oiled clingfilm and leave in a warm place for about 40 minutes until doubled in size.

Bake in a preheated oven at 220°C/ 425°F/gas mark 7 for 10–15 minutes until hollow-sounding when tapped on the base.

Granary Bread with Hazelnuts

Makes one 900 g/2 lb loaf

15 g/½ oz fresh yeast or 20 ml/ 4 tsp dried yeast

5 ml/1 tsp soft brown sugar

450 ml/¾ pt/2 cups warm water

450 g/1 lb/4 cups granary flour

175 g/6 oz/1½ cups strong plain (bread) flour

5 ml/1 tsp salt

15 ml/1 tbsp olive oil

100 g/4 oz/1 cup hazelnuts, coarsely chopped

Blend the yeast with the sugar and a little of the warm water and leave in a warm place for 20 minutes until frothy. Mix together the flours and salt in a bowl, add the yeast mixture, the oil and the remaining warm water and mix to a firm dough. Knead until smooth and no longer sticky. Place in an oiled bowl, cover with oiled clingfilm (plastic wrap) and leave in a warm place for about 1 hour until doubled in size.

Knead again lightly and work in the nuts, then shape into a greased 900 g/2 lb loaf tin (pan), cover with oiled clingfilm and leave in a warm place for 30 minutes until the dough has risen above the top of the tin.

Bake in a preheated oven at 220°C/ 425°F/gas mark 7 for 30 minutes until golden brown and hollow-sounding when tapped on the base.

Grissini

Makes 12

25 g/1 oz fresh yeast or 40 ml/ 2½ tbsp dried yeast

15 ml/1 tbsp caster (superfine) sugar

120 ml/4 fl oz/½ cup warm milk

25 g/1 oz/2 tbsp butter or margarine

450 g/1 lb/4 cups strong plain (bread) flour

10 ml/2 tsp salt

Blend the yeast with 5 ml/1 tsp of the sugar and a little of the warm milk and leave in a warm place for 20 minutes until frothy. Melt the butter and remaining sugar in the remaining warm milk. Place the flour and salt in a bowl and make a well in the centre. Pour in the yeast and milk mixture and combine to make a moist dough. Knead until smooth. Place in an oiled bowl, cover with oiled clingfilm (plastic wrap) and leave in a warm place for about 1 hour until doubled in size.

Knead lightly, then divide into 12 and roll out into long, thin sticks and place, well apart, on a greased baking (cookie) sheet. Cover with oiled clingfilm and leave to rise in a warm place for 20 minutes.

Brush the bread sticks with water, then bake in a preheated oven at 220°C/425°F/ gas mark 7 for 10 minutes, then reduce the oven temperature to 180°C/350°F/ gas mark 4 and bake for a further 20 minutes until crisp.

Harvest Plait

Makes one 550 g/1¼ lb loaf

25 g/1 oz fresh yeast or 40 ml/ 2½ tbsp dried yeast

25 g/1 oz/2 tbsp caster (superfine) sugar

150 ml/¼ pt/2/3 cup warm milk

50 g/2 oz/¼ cup butter or margarine, melted

1 egg, beaten

450 g/1 lb/4 cups plain (all-purpose) flour

A pinch of salt

30 ml/2 tbsp currants

2.5 ml/½ tsp of ground cinnamon

5 ml/1 tsp grated lemon rind

Milk for glazing

Blend the yeast with 2.5 ml/½ tsp of the sugar and a little of the warm milk and leave in a warm place for about 20 minutes until frothy. Mix the remaining milk with the butter or margarine and leave to cool slightly. Mix in the egg. Place the remaining ingredients in a bowl and make a well in the centre. Stir in the milk and yeast mixtures and mix to a soft dough. Knead until elastic and no longer sticky. Place in an oiled bowl and cover with oiled clingfilm (plastic wrap). Leave in a warm place for about 1 hour until doubled in size.

Divide the dough into three and roll into strips. Moisten one end of each strip and seal the ends together, then plait them together and moisten and secure the other ends. Place on a greased baking (cookie) sheet, cover with oiled clingfilm and leave in a warm place for 15 minutes.

Brush with a little milk and bake in a preheated oven at 220°C/425°F/gas mark 7 for 15–20 minutes until golden brown and hollow-sounding when tapped on the base.

Milk Bread

Makes two 450 g/1 lb loaves

15 g/½ oz fresh yeast or 20 ml/ 4 tsp dried yeast

5 ml/1 tsp caster (superfine) sugar

450 ml/¾ pt/2 cups warm milk

50 g/2 oz/¼ cup butter or margarine

675 g/1½ lb/6 cups plain (all-purpose) flour

A pinch of salt

Milk for glazing

Blend the yeast with the sugar and a little of the warm milk. Leave to stand in a warm place for about 20 minutes until frothy. Rub the butter or margarine into the flour and salt and make a well in the centre. Mix in the remaining warm milk and the yeast mixture and knead to a soft but not sticky dough. Place in an oiled bowl and cover with oiled clingfilm (plastic wrap). Leave in a warm place for about 1 hour until doubled in size.

Knead again lightly, then divide the mixture between two greased 450 g/1 lb loaf tins (pans), cover with oiled clingfilm and leave to rise for about 15 minutes until the dough is just above the tops of the tins.

Brush with a little milk, then bake in a preheated oven at 200°C/400°F/gas mark 6 for 30 minutes until golden brown and hollow-sounding when tapped on the base.

Milk Fruit Loaf

Makes two 450 g/1 lb loaves

15 g/½ oz fresh yeast or 20 ml/ 4 tsp dried yeast

5 ml/1 tsp caster (superfine) sugar

450 ml/¾ pt/2 cups warm milk

50 g/2 oz/¼ cup butter or margarine

675 g/1½ lb/6 cups plain (all-purpose) flour

A pinch of salt

100 g/4 oz/2/3 cup raisins

Milk for glazing

Blend the yeast with the sugar and a little of the warm milk. Leave to stand in a warm place for about 20 minutes until frothy. Rub the butter or margarine into the flour and salt, stir in the raisins and make a well in the centre. Mix in the remaining warm milk and the yeast mixture and knead to a soft but not sticky dough. Place in an oiled bowl and cover with oiled clingfilm (plastic wrap). Leave in a warm place for about 1 hour until doubled in size.

Knead again lightly, then divide the mixture between two greased 450 g/1 lb loaf tins (pans), cover with oiled clingfilm and leave to rise for about 15 minutes until the dough is just above the tops of the tins.

Brush with a little milk, then bake in a preheated oven at 200°C/400°F/gas mark 6 for 30 minutes until golden brown and hollow-sounding when tapped on the base.

Morning Glory Bread

Makes two 450 g/1 lb loaves

100 g/4 oz/1 cup whole wheat grains

15 ml/1 tbsp malt extract

450 ml/¾ pt/2 cups warm water

25 g/1 oz fresh yeast or 40 ml/ 2½ tbsp dried yeast

30 ml/2 tbsp clear honey

25 g/1 oz/2 tbsp vegetable fat (shortening)

675 g/1½ lb/6 cups wholemeal (wholewheat) flour

25 g/1 oz/¼ cup milk powder (non-fat dry milk)

5 ml/1 tsp salt

Soak the whole wheat grains and malt extract in the warm water overnight.

Blend the yeast with a little more warm water and 5 ml/1 tsp of the honey. Leave in a warm place for about 20 minutes until frothy. Rub the fat into the flour, milk powder and salt and make a well in the centre. Stir in the yeast mixture, the remaining honey and the wheat mixture and mix to a dough. Knead well until smooth and no longer sticky. Place in an oiled bowl, cover with oiled clingfilm (plastic wrap) and leave in a warm place for about 1 hour until doubled in size.

Knead the dough again, then shape into two greased 450 g/1 lb loaf tins (pans). Cover with oiled clingfilm and leave in a warm place for 40 minutes until the dough reaches just above the tops of the tins.

Bake in a preheated oven at 200°C/ 425°F/gas mark 7 for about 25 minutes until well risen and hollow-sounding when tapped on the base.

Muffin Bread

Makes two 900 g/2 lb loaves

300 g/10 oz/2½ cups wholemeal (wholewheat) flour

300 g/10 oz/2½ cups plain (all-purpose) flour

40 ml/2½ tbsp dried yeast

15 ml/1 tbsp caster (superfine) sugar

10 ml/2 tsp salt

500 ml/17 fl oz/2¼ cups lukewarm milk

2.5 ml/½ tsp bicarbonate of soda (baking soda)

15 ml/1 tbsp warm water

Mix the flours together. Measure 350 g/12 oz/3 cups of the mixed flours into a bowl and mix in the yeast, sugar and salt. Stir in the milk and beat to a stiff mixture. Mix together the bicarbonate of soda and water and stir into the dough with the remaining flour. Divide the mixture between two greased 900 g/2 lb loaf tins (pans), cover and leave to rise for about 1 hour until doubled in size.

Bake in a preheated oven at 190°C/ 375°F/gas mark 5 for 1¼ hours until well risen and golden brown.

No-rise Bread

Makes one 900 g/2 lb loaf

450 g/1 lb/4 cups wholemeal (wholewheat) flour

175 g/6 oz/1½ cups self-raising (self-rising) flour

5 ml/1 tsp salt

30 ml/2 tbsp caster (superfine) sugar

450 ml/¾ pt/2 cups milk

20 ml/4 tsp vinegar

30 ml/2 tbsp oil

5 ml/1 tsp bicarbonate of soda (baking soda)

Mix together the flours, salt and sugar and make a well in the centre. Beat together the milk, vinegar, oil and bicarbonate of soda, pour into the dry ingredients and blend to a smooth dough. Shape into a greased 900 g/2 lb loaf tin (pan) and bake in a preheated oven at 180°C/350°F/gas mark 4 for 1 hour until golden brown and hollow-sounding when tapped on the base.

Pizza Dough

Makes enough for two 23 cm/9 in pizzas

15 g/½ oz fresh yeast or 20 ml/ 4 tsp dried yeast

A pinch of sugar

250 ml/8 fl oz/1 cup warm water

350 g/12 oz/3 cups plain (all-purpose) flour

A pinch of salt

30 ml/2 tbsp olive oil

Blend the yeast with the sugar and a little of the warm water and leave in a warm place for 20 minutes until frothy. Blend into the flour with the salt and olive oil and knead until smooth and no longer sticky. Place in an oiled bowl, cover with oiled clingfilm (plastic wrap) and leave in a warm place for 1 hour until doubled in size. Knead again and shape as required.

Oatmeal Cob

Makes one 450 g/1 lb loaf

25 g/1 oz fresh yeast or 40 ml/ 2½ tbsp dried yeast

5 ml/1 tsp caster (superfine) sugar

150 ml/¼ pt/2/3 cup lukewarm milk

150 ml/¼ pt/2/3 cup lukewarm water

400 g/14 oz/3½ cups strong plain (bread) flour

5 ml/1 tsp salt

25 g/1 oz/2 tbsp butter or margarine

100 g/4 oz/1 cup medium oatmeal

Blend the yeast and sugar with the milk and water and leave in a warm place until frothy. Mix together the flour and salt, then rub in the butter or margarine and stir in the oatmeal. Make a well in the centre, pour in the yeast mixture and mix to a soft dough. Turn out on a floured surface and knead for 10 minutes until smooth and elastic. Place in an oiled bowl, cover with oiled clingfilm (plastic wrap) and leave in a warm place to rise for about 1 hour until doubled in size.

Knead the dough again, then shape into a loaf shape of your choice. Place on a greased baking (cookie) sheet, brush with a little water, cover with oiled clingfilm and leave in a warm place for about 40 minutes until doubled in size.

Bake in a preheated oven at 230°C/ 450°F/gas mark 8 for 25 minutes until well risen and golden brown and hollow-sounding when tapped on the base.

Oatmeal Farl

Makes 4

25 g/1 oz fresh yeast or 40 ml/ 2½ tbsp dried yeast

5 ml/1 tsp honey

300 ml/½ pt/1¼ cups warm water

450 g/1 lb/4 cups strong plain (bread) flour

50 g/2 oz/½ cup medium oatmeal

2.5 ml/½ tsp baking powder

A pinch of salt

25 g/1 oz/2 tbsp butter or margarine

Blend the yeast with the honey and a little of the warm water and leave in a warm place for 20 minutes until frothy.

Mix together the flour, oatmeal, baking powder and salt and rub in the butter or margarine. Stir in the yeast mixture and the remaining warm water and mix to a medium-soft dough. Knead until elastic and no longer sticky. Place in an oiled bowl, cover with oiled clingfilm (plastic wrap) and leave in a warm place for about 1 hour until doubled in size.

Knead again lightly and shape into a round about 3 cm/1¼ in thick. Cut across into quarters and place, slightly apart but still in the original round shape, on a greased baking (cookie) sheet. Cover with oiled clingfilm and leave to rise for about 30 minutes until doubled in size.

Bake in a preheated oven at 200°C/ 400°F/gas mark 6 for 30 minutes until golden brown and hollow-sounding when tapped on the base.

Pitta Bread

Makes 6

15 g/½ oz fresh yeast or 20 ml/ 4 tsp dried yeast

5 ml/1 tsp caster (superfine) sugar

300 ml/½ pt/1¼ cups warm water

450 g/1 lb/4 cups strong plain (bread) flour

5 ml/1 tsp salt

Blend together the yeast, sugar and a little of the warm water and leave in a warm place for 20 minutes until frothy. Blend the yeast mixture and remaining warm water into the flour and salt and mix to a firm dough. Knead until smooth and elastic. Place in an oiled bowl, cover with oiled clingfilm (plastic wrap) and leave in a warm place for about 1 hour until doubled in size.

Knead again and divide into six pieces. Roll into ovals about 5 mm/¼ in thick and place on a greased baking (cookie) sheet. Cover with oiled clingfilm and leave to rise for 40 minutes until doubled in size.

Bake in a preheated oven at 230°C/ 450°F/gas mark 8 for 10 minutes until lightly golden.

Quick Brown Bread

Makes two 450 g/1 lb loaves

15 g/½ oz fresh yeast or 20 ml/ 4 tsp dried yeast

300 ml/½ pt/1¼ cups warm milk and water mixed

15 ml/1 tbsp black treacle (molasses)

225 g/8 oz/2 cups wholemeal (wholewheat) flour

225 g/8 oz/2 cups plain (all-purpose) flour

10 ml/2 tsp salt

25 g/1 oz/2 tbsp butter or margarine

15 ml/1 tbsp cracked wheat

Blend the yeast with a little warm milk and water and the treacle and leave in a warm place until frothy. Mix the flours and salt and rub in the butter or margarine. Make a well in the centre and pour in the yeast mixture, blending to a firm dough. Turn out on to a floured surface and knead for 10 minutes until smooth and elastic, or process in a food processor. Shape into two loaves and place in greased and lined 450 g/1 lb loaf tins (pans). Brush the tops with water and sprinkle with the cracked wheat. Cover with oiled clingfilm (plastic wrap) and leave in a warm place for about 1 hour until doubled in size.

Bake in a preheated oven at 240°C/ 475°F/gas mark 8 for 40 minutes until the loaves sound hollow when tapped on the base.

Moist Rice Bread

Makes one 900 g/2 lb loaf

75 g/3 oz/1/3 cup long-grain rice

15 g/½ oz fresh yeast or 20 ml/ 4 tsp dried yeast

A pinch of sugar

250 ml/8 fl oz/1 cup warm water

550 g/1¼ lb/5 cups strong plain (bread) flour

2.5 ml/½ tsp salt

Measure the rice into a cup, then pour into a pan. Add three times the volume of cold water, bring to the boil, cover and simmer for about 20 minutes until the water has been absorbed. Meanwhile blend the yeast with the sugar and a little of the warm water and leave in a warm place for 20 minutes until frothy.

Place the flour and salt in a bowl and make a well in the centre. Blend in the yeast mixture and the warm rice and mix to a soft dough. Place in an oiled bowl, cover with oiled clingfilm (plastic wrap) and leave in a warm place for about 1 hour until doubled in size.

Knead lightly, adding a little more flour if the dough is too soft to work, and shape into a greased 900 g/2 lb loaf tin (pan). Cover with oiled clingfilm and leave in a warm place for 30 minutes until the dough has risen above the top of the tin.

Bake in a preheated oven at 230°C/ 450°F/gas mark 8 for 10 minutes, then reduce the oven temperature to 200°C/ 400°F/gas mark 6 and bake for a further 25 minutes until golden brown and hollow-sounding when tapped on the base.

Rice and Almond Loaf

Makes one 900 g/2 lb loaf

175 g/6 oz/¾ cup butter or margarine, softened

175 g/6 oz/¾ cup caster (superfine) sugar

3 eggs, lightly beaten

100 g/4 oz/1 cup strong plain (bread) flour

5 ml/1 tsp baking powder

A pinch of salt

100 g/4 oz/1 cup ground rice

50 g/2 oz/½ cup ground almonds

15 ml/1 tbsp warm water

Cream together the butter or mar-garine and sugar until light and fluffy. Gradually beat in the eggs, then fold in the dry ingredients and the water to make a smooth dough. Shape into a greased 900 g/2 lb loaf tin (pan) and bake in a preheated oven at 180°C/350°F/gas mark 4 for 1 hour until golden brown and hollow-sounding when tapped on the base.

Crunchy Rusks

Makes 24

675 g/1½ lb/6 cups plain (all-purpose) flour

15 ml/1 tbsp cream of tartar

10 ml/2 tsp salt

400 g/14 oz/1¾ cups caster (superfine) sugar

250 g/9 oz/generous 1 cup butter or margarine

10 ml/2 tsp bicarbonate of soda (baking soda)

250 ml/8 fl oz/1 cup buttermilk

1 egg

Mix together the flour, cream of tartar and salt. Stir in the sugar.
Rub in the butter or margarine until the mixture resembles
breadcrumbs and make a well in the centre. Mix the bicarbonate of
soda with a little of the buttermilk, and mix the egg into the
remaining buttermilk. Reserve 30 ml/2 tbsp of the egg mixture to
glaze the rusks. Mix the remainder into the dry ingredients with
the bicarbonate of soda mixture and blend to a stiff dough. Divide
the dough into six equal portions and shape into sausages. Flatten
slightly and cut each one into six pieces. Arrange on a greased
baking (cookie) sheet and brush with the reserved egg mixture.
Bake in a preheated oven at 200°C/400°F/gas mark 6 for 30
minute until golden brown.

Rye Bread

Makes two 450 g/1 lb loaves

25 g/1 oz fresh yeast or 40 ml/ 2½ tbsp dried yeast

15 ml/1 tbsp soft brown sugar

300 ml/½ pt/1¼ cups warm water

450 g/1 lb/4 cups rye flour

225 g/8 oz/2 cups strong (bread) flour

5 ml/1 tsp salt

5 ml/1 tsp caraway seeds

150 ml/¼ pt/2/3 cup warm milk

Blend the yeast with the sugar and a little of the warm water and leave in a warm place until frothy. Mix together the flours, salt and caraway seeds and make a well in the centre. Mix in the yeast mixture, the milk and remaining water and mix to a firm dough. Turn out on a floured surface and knead for 8 minutes until smooth and elastic, or process in a food processor. Place in an oiled bowl, cover with oiled clingfilm (plastic wrap) and leave in a warm place for about 1 hour until doubled in size. Knead again, then shape into two loaves and place on a greased baking (cookie) sheet. Cover with oiled clingfilm and leave to rise for 30 minutes.

Bake in a preheated oven at 220°C/ 425°F/gas mark 7 for 15 minutes, then reduce the oven temperature to 190°C/ 375°F/gas mark 5 for a further 25 minutes until the loaves sound hollow when tapped on the base.

CPSIA information can be obtained
at www.ICGtesting.com
Printed in the USA
LVHW081814010621
689062LV00015B/1753

9 781802 904482